BITE-SIZE
TWAIN

BITE-SIZE
TWAIN

Wit & Wisdom
from the Literary Legend

COMPILED BY JOHN P. HOLMS AND KARIN BAJI

ST. MARTIN'S PRESS ☙ NEW YORK

BITE-SIZE TWAIN: WIT & WISDOM FROM THE LITERARY LEGEND. Copyright © 1998 by John P. Holms and Karin Baji. All rights reserved. Printed in the United States of America. No part of this book may be used or reproduced in any manner whatsoever without written permission except in the case of brief quotations embodied in critical articles or reviews. For information, address St. Martin's Press, 175 Fifth Avenue, New York, N.Y. 10010.

Production Editor: David Stanford Burr

Design: Bryanna Millis

Library of Congress Cataloging-in-Publication Data

Twain, Mark, 1835–1910.
    Bite-size Twain : wit & wisdom from the literary legend / compiled by John P. Holms and Karin Baji.—1st ed.
        p.   cm.
    "A Thomas Dunne book."
    ISBN 0-312-19087-5
    1. Twain, Mark, 1835–1910—Quotations.   2. Quotations, American.   I. Holms, John P., 1944–   .   II. Baji, Karin. III. Title.
PS1303.H565   1998
818'.402—dc21   98-11232
                                                                              CIP

First Edition: July 1998

10   9   8   7   6   5   4   3   2   1

GRATEFUL THANKS TO MR. CLEMENS,

TO PETE WOLVERTON, TO TOM DUNNE AND,

OF COURSE, LEFTY, A DACHSHUND WHO LOVES

LONG HALLWAYS AND IS A GREAT NEGOTIATOR.

Contents

Ah, well, I am a great and sublime fool. But then I am God's fool, and all his works must be contemplated with respect.

Twain on Twain

I have been born more times than anybody except Krishna.

My mother had a good deal of trouble with me, but I think she enjoyed it. She had none at all with my brother, Henry, who was two years younger than I, and I think that the unbroken monotony of his goodness and truthfulness and obedience would have been a burden to her but for the relief and variety which I furnished in the other direction. I was a tonic. I was valuable to her.

I ran away twice; once at about 13, and once at 17. There is not much satisfaction in it, even as a recollection. It was a couple of disappointments, particularly the first one. The heroics squish out of such things so promptly.

I was born modest; not all over, but in spots.

I am the whole human race without a detail lacking; I have studied the human race with diligence and strong interest all these years in my own person, in myself. I find in big or little proportion every quality and every defect that is findable in the mass of the race.

I must have a prodigious quantity of mind; it takes me as much as a week to make it up.

I was seldom able to see an opportunity until it had ceased to be one.

[Twain applies for a German passport in 1878 and describes himself to the authorities] My description is as follows: Born 1835; 5 ft. 8½ inches tall; weight about 145 pounds . . . dark brown hair and red moustache, full face with very high ears and light gray beautiful beaming eyes and a damned good moral character.

I was always handsome. Anybody but a critic could have seen it.

I am an old man and have known a great many troubles, but most of them never happened.

My memory was never loaded with anything but blank cartridges.

I have always been able to gain my living without doing any work; for the writing of books and magazine matter was always play, not work. I enjoyed it; it was merely billiards to me.

[William Dean Howells] did me the justice to say that my intentions were always good, that I wounded people's conventions rather than their convictions. I would rather wait, with anything harsh I might have to say, till the convictions become conventions.

Yes, you are right—I am a moralist in disguise; it gets me into heaps of trouble when I go thrashing around in political questions.

I have always preached. . . . If the humor came of its own accord and uninvited, I have allowed it a place in my sermon, but I was not writing the sermon for the sake of the humor.

Part of my plan has been to pleasantly remind adults of what they were themselves, and of how they felt and thought and talked, and what queer enterprises they sometimes engaged in.

It has been reported that I was seriously ill—it was another man; dying—it was another man; dead—the other man again. . . . As far as I can see, nothing remains to be reported, except that I have become a foreigner. When you hear it, don't you believe it. And don't take the trouble to deny it. Merely just raise the American flag on our house in Hartford and let it talk.

I—well I was an exception, you understand—my kind don't turn up every day. We are very rare. We are a sort

of human century plant, and we don't blossom in everybody's front yard.

The story of my life will make certain people sit up and take notice, but I will use my influence not to have it published until the persons mentioned in it and their children and grandchildren are dead. I tell you it will be something awful. It will be what you might call good reading.

I came in with Halley's Comet in 1835. It is coming again next year, and I expect to go out with it. It will be the greatest disappointment of my life if I don't go out with Halley's Comet. The Almighty has said, no doubt: "Now here are these two unaccountable freaks; they came in together, they must go out together."

Ah, well, I am a great and sublime fool. But then I am God's fool, and all his works must be contemplated with respect.

On Americans

We are called the nation of inventors. And we are. We could still claim that title and wear its loftiest honors if we had stopped with the first thing we ever invented, which was human liberty.

I think that the reason why we Americans seem to be so addicted to trying to get rich suddenly is merely because the opportunity to make promising efforts in that direction has offered itself to us with a frequency all out of proportion to the European experience.

Ours is the "land of the free"—nobody denies that—nobody challenges it. (Maybe it is because we won't let other people testify.)

My first American ancestor, gentleman, was an Indian—an early Indian. Your ancestors skinned him alive. . . . All those Salem witches were ancestors of mine. Your people made it tropical for them. . . . The first slave

brought into New England out of Africa by your progenitors was an ancestor of mine—for I am a mixed breed, an infinitely shaded and exquisite Mongrel.

It was wonderful to find America, but it would have been more wonderful to miss it.

> [In Genoa, Twain speaks to a guide pointing to a bust of Christopher Columbus] "Ah, what did you say this gentleman's name was?"
> "Christopher Colombo!—great Christopher Colombo!"
> "Christopher Colombo—the great Christopher Colombo. Well, what did *he* do?"
> "Discover America!—discover America, Oh, ze devil!"
> "Discover America. No—that statement will hardly wash. We are just from America ourselves. We heard nothing about it. Christopher Colombo—pleasant name—is—is he dead?"

The world and the books are so accustomed to use, and over-use, the word "new" in connection with our country, that we early get and permanently retain the impression that there is nothing old about it.

An Englishman is a person who does things because they have been done before. An American is a person who does things because they haven't been done before.

I think that as a rule we develop a borrowed European idea forward and that Europe develops a borrowed American idea backwards.

In America . . . we scoff at titles and hereditary privilege but privately we hanker after them, and when we get a chance we buy them for cash and a daughter.

God was left out of the Constitution but was furnished a front seat on the coins of the country.

The motto ("In God We Trust") stated a lie. If this nation ever trusted in God, that time has gone by;

for nearly half a century its entire trust has been in the Republican Party and the dollar—mainly the dollar.

In Boston they ask, How much does he know? In New York, How much is he worth? In Philadelphia, Who were his parents?

The coldest winter I ever spent was a summer in San Francisco.—*attributed*

There is a sumptuous variety about the New England weather. . . . In the spring I have counted one hundred thirty-six different kinds of weather inside of four and twenty hours.

We asked a passenger who belonged there what sort of place [Arkansas] was. "Well," said he, after considering, and with the air of one who wishes to take time and be accurate, "It's a hell of a place." A description which was photographic for exactness.

[The Duke makes handbills for his troop's performance of Shakespeare, and puts only one line in capital letters . . .] "'LADIES AND CHILDREN NOT ADMITTED.'" There . . . if that line don't fetch them, I don't know Arkansas!"—*Adventures of Huckleberry Finn* (1884)

The educated Southerner has no use for an r, except at the beginning of a word.

In the South the war is what A.D. is elsewhere; they date from it.

ON BOYHOOD

We were good Presbyterian boys when the weather was doubtful. When it was fair we did wander a little from the fold.

He was not the Model Boy of the village. He knew the model boy very well though—and loathed him.

The Model Boy of my time—we never had but the one—was perfect; perfect in manners, perfect in dress, perfect in conduct, perfect in filial piety, perfect in exterior godliness . . . he was the admiration of all the mothers and the detestation of all their sons.

When I was younger I could remember anything, whether it happened or not.

[On George Washington] He was ignorant of the commonest accomplishments of youth. He could not even lie.

Now and then we had a hope that if we lived and were good, God would permit us to be pirates.

There comes a time in every rightly constructed boy's life when he has a raging desire to go somewhere and dig for hidden treasure.

It is a wise child that knows its own father and an unusual one that unreservedly approves of him.

Schoolboy days are no happier than the days of afterlife, but we look back upon them regretfully because we have forgotten our punishments at school and how we grieved when our marbles were lost and our kites destroyed—because we have forgotten all the sorrows and privations of that canonized epoch and remember only its orchard robberies, its wooden-sword pageants, and its fishing holidays.

On Censorship

The mind that becomes soiled in youth can never again be washed clean; I know this by my own experience, and to this day I cherish an unappeasable bitterness against the unfaithful guardians of my young life, who not only permitted but compelled me to read an unexpurgated Bible through before I was fifteen years old.

Most honestly do I wish that I could say a softening word or two in defense of Huck's character since you wish it, but really, in my opinion, it is no better than those of Solomon, David, and the rest of the sacred brotherhood.

The Committee of the Public Library of Concord, Mass. [has] expelled Huck from their library as "trash and suitable only for the slums." That will sell 25,000 copies for us for sure.

On Clothes

Clothes make the man. Naked people have little or no influence on society.

We must put up with our clothes as they are—they have their reason for existing. They are on us to expose us—to advertise what we wear them to conceal. They are a sign; a sign of insincerity; a sign of suppressed vanity; a pretense that we desire gorgeous colors and the graces of harmony and form; and we put them on to propagate that lie and back it up.

Modesty died when clothes were born.

Be careless in your dress if you must, but keep a tidy soul.

A policeman in plain clothes is a man; in his uniform he is ten. Clothes and title are the most potent thing, the most formidable influence, on the earth. They move the human race to willing and spontaneous respect for the judge, the general, the admiral, the bishop, the ambassador, the frivolous earl, the idiot duke, the sultan, the king, the emperor. No great title is efficient without clothes to support it.

No woman can look as well out of the fashion as in it.

Some civilized women would lose half their charm without dress and some would lose all of it.

On Conversation & Manners

Truth is good manners; manners are a fiction.

It is better to keep your mouth shut and appear stupid than to open it and remove all doubt.

Good breeding consists of concealing how much we think of ourselves and how little we think of the other person.

A banquet is probably the most fatiguing thing in the world except ditchdigging.

The man who is ostentatious of his modesty is twin to the statue that wears the fig-leaf.

No real gentleman will tell the naked truth in the presence of the ladies.

The highest perfection of politeness is only a beautiful edifice, built, from the base to the dome, of graceful and gilded forms of charitable and unselfish lying.

KINDNESS
Kindness is the language which the deaf can hear and the blind can see.

PAYING COMPLIMENTS
Do not offer a compliment and ask a favor at the same time. A compliment that is charged for is not valuable.

I can live for two months on a good compliment.

I think a compliment ought always to precede a complaint, where one is possible, because it softens resentment and insures for the complaint a courteous and gentle reception.

I have been complimented myself a great many times, and they always embarrass me—I always feel they have not said enough.

CRITICISM

Always acknowledge a fault frankly. This will throw those in authority off their guard and give you an opportunity to commit more.

You must not pay a person a compliment, and then straightway follow it with a criticism.

I like criticism, but it must be my way.

One mustn't criticize other people on grounds where he can't stand perpendicular himself.

GOSSIP

Rumor will die itself if you will only give it three days. Start any rumor, and if the public can go with its curiosity unsatisfied for three days something else will spring up which will make the public forget all about the first one.

There is a lot to say in her favor, but the other is more interesting.

On Correspondence

How wonderful are old letters in bringing a dead past back to life and filling it with movement and stir of figures clothed in ruddy flesh! It all seems more real and present than it does in a novel, and one feels it more and is more a part of it, with the joy light in one's eyes, and one's own heart on the skewer.

When you get an exasperating letter what happens? If you are young, you answer it promptly, instantly—and mail the thing you have written. At forty what do you do? By that time you have found out that a letter written in passion is a mistake in ninety-nine cases out of a hundred.

An old, cold letter . . . makes you wonder how you could ever have got into such a rage about nothing.

The reason I dread writing letters is because I am so apt to get to slinging wisdom and forget to let up. Thus much precious time is lost. The most useful and interesting letters we get here from home are from children seven or eight years old. . . . They write simply and naturally and without strain for effect. They tell all they know, and stop.

ON CREATION

Man—a creature made at the end of the week's work when God was tired.

Where was the use, originally, in rushing this whole globe through in six days? It is likely that if more time had been taken in the first place, the world would have been made right, and this ceaseless improving and repairing would not be necessary now. But if you hurry a world or a house, you are nearly sure to find out by and by that you have left out a towhead, or a broom-closet, or some other little convenience, here and there, which has got to be supplied, no matter how much expense or vexation it may cost.

I believe that our Heavenly Father invented man because he was disappointed in the monkey.

If man had created man he would be ashamed of his performance.

Adam was but human—this explains it all. He did not want the apple for the apple's sake; he wanted it only because it was forbidden. The mistake was in not forbidding the serpent; then he would have eaten the serpent.

Such is the human race . . . often it seems a pity that Noah and his party didn't miss the boat.

Of all the creatures that were made he [man] is the most detestable. Of the entire brood he is the only one—that possesses malice. That is the basest of all instincts, passions, vices—the most hateful. . . . He is the only creature that inflicts pain for sport, knowing it to *be* pain. . . . Also—in all the list he is the only creature that has a nasty mind.

Adam was the author of sin, and I wish he had taken out an international copyright on it.

Nothing is made in vain, but the fly came near it.

On Custom

Often, the less there is to justify a traditional custom, the harder it is to get rid of it.

Custom is a petrifaction; nothing but dynamite can dislodge it for a century.

A crime persevered in a thousand centuries ceases to be a crime, and becomes a virtue. This is the law of custom, and custom supersedes all other forms of law.

Have a place for everything and keep the thing somewhere else; this is not advice, it is merely custom.

There isn't anything you can't stand, if you are only born and bred to it.

Laws are sand, customs are rock. Laws can be evaded and punishment escaped, but an openly transgressed custom brings sure punishment.

On Doing Right

Always do right—this will gratify some and astonish the rest.

Few things are harder to put up with than the annoyance of a good example.

Be good and you will be lonesome.

To be good is noble; but to show others how to be good is nobler and no trouble.

Each man must for himself alone decide what is right and what is wrong, which course is patriotic and which isn't. You cannot shirk this and be a man. To decide against your conviction is to be an unqualified and excusable traitor, both to yourself and to your country, let men label you as they may.

Alas, if we but do right under restraint of authoritative observance, where then is the merit?

Always obey your parents, when they are present. Most parents think they know more than you do; and you can generally make more by humoring that superstition than you can by acting on your own better judgment.

It is good to obey all the rules when you're young, so you'll have the strength to break them when you're old.

We can secure other people's approval if we do right and try hard; but our own is worth a hundred of it, and no way has been found out of securing that.

ON EDUCATION

Education consists mainly in what we have unlearned.

Education is what you must acquire without any interference from your schooling.

The man who doesn't read good books has no advantage over the man who can't read them.

In the first place, God made idiots. That was for practice. Then he made schoolboards.

When I was a boy on the Mississippi River there was a proposition in a township there to discontinue public schools because they were too expensive. An old farmer spoke up and said if they stopped the schools they would not save anything, because every time a school was closed a jail had to be built.

Out of the public schools grows the greatness of a nation.

ON FAME

To some people it is fatal to be recognized by greatness.

Fame is a vapor; popularity an accident; the only earthly certainty is oblivion.

Obscurity and a competence. That is the life that is best worth living.

Reputation is a hall-mark: it can remove doubt from pure silver, and it can also make the plated article pass for pure.

Robert Louis Stevenson and I, sitting in Union Square and Washington Square a great many years ago, tried to find a name for, the submerged fame, that fame that permeates the great crowd of people you never see and never mingle with; people with whom you have no speech, but who read your books and become admirers of your work and have an affection for you. You may never find it out in the world, but there it is, and it is the faithfulness of the friendship, of the homage of those men, never criticizing, that began when they were children. They have nothing but compliments, they never see the criticisms, they never hear any disparagement of you, and you will remain in the home of their hearts' affection forever and ever. And Louis Stevenson and I decided that of all fame, that was the best, the very best.

On Friends & Foes

The holy passion of Friendship is of so sweet and steady and loyal and enduring a nature that it will last through a whole lifetime, if not asked to lend money.

Good friends, good books and a sleepy conscience: this is the ideal life.

It takes your enemy and your friend, working together, to hurt you to the heart; the one to slander you and the other to get the news to you.

The proper office of a friend is to side with you when you are in the wrong. Nearly everybody will side with you when you are in the right.

That a person can really be a hero to a near and familiar friend is a thing which no hero has ever yet been able to realize.

ON GROWING OLD

When I was a boy of fourteen, my father was so ignorant I could hardly stand to have the old man around. But when I got to be twenty-one, I was astonished at how much the old man had learned in seven years.

The man who is a pessimist before forty-eight knows too much; if he is an optimist after it, he knows too little.

Wrinkles should merely indicate where smiles have been.

A man never reaches that dizzy height of wisdom that he can no longer be led by the nose.

There has never been an intelligent person of the age of sixty who would consent to live his life over again. His or anyone else's.

Life would be infinitely happier if we could only be born at the age of eighty and gradually approach eighteen.

It takes some time to accept and realize that while you have been growing old, your friends have not been standing still in that matter.

It isn't so astonishing, the number of things that I can remember, as the number of things I can remember that aren't so.

—

The natural way provided by nature and the construction of the human mind for the discovery of a forgotten event is to employ another forgotten event for its resurrection.

[Twain's seventieth birthday speech, 1905] And I wish to urge you this—which I think is wisdom—that if you find you can't make seventy by any but an uncomfortable road, don't you go.

Take any road you please . . . it curves always, which is a continual promise, whereas straight roads reveal everything at a glance and kill interest.

We can't reach old age by another man's road. My habits protect my life but they would assassinate you.

On Health & Fitness

Be careful about reading health books. You may die of a misprint.

> *To eat is human*
> *To digest divine.*

Part of the secret success in life is to eat what you like and let the food fight it out inside.

Nothing helps scenery like ham and eggs.

I have never taken any exercise except sleeping and resting, and I never intend to take any. Exercise is loathsome.

In the matter of diet—I have been persistently strict in sticking to the things which didn't agree with me until one or the other of us got the best of it.

Sometimes too much to drink is barely enough.

———

Water, taken in moderation, cannot hurt anybody.

[Twain remarks how easy it is to give up smoking] I've done it a hundred times!

It has always been my rule never to smoke when asleep, and never to refrain when awake.

A good and wholesome thing is a little harmless fun in this world; it tones a body up and keeps him human and prevents him from souring.

Lecturing is gymnastics, chest-expander, medicine, mind-healer, blues-destroyer, all in one.

The only way to keep your health is to eat what you don't want, drink what you don't like, and do what you'd rather not.

What, then, is the grand result of all this microbing and sanitation and surgery? . . . In time there will not be room in the world for the people to stand, let alone sit down.

There are people who strictly deprive themselves of each and every eatable, drinkable, and smokable which has in any way acquired a shady reputation. They pay this price for health. And health is all they get for it. How strange it is. It is like paying out your whole fortune for a cow that has gone dry.

O N   H E A V E N   &   H E L L

What a hell of a heaven it will be when they get all these hypocrites assembled there!

She went on and told me all about the good place. She said all a body would have to do there was to go around all day long with a harp and sing, forever and ever. So I didn't think much of it.—*Adventures of Huckleberry Finn* (1884)

Heaven for climate, hell for society.

The first time the Deity came down to earth, he brought life and death; when he came the second time, he brought hell.

When I think of the number of disagreeable people that I know who have gone to a better world, I am sure hell won't be so bad at all.

Heaven goes by favor. If it went by merit, you would stay out and your dog would go in.

ON IMAGINATION

You can't depend on your eyes when you're imagination is out of focus.

Keep away from people who try to belittle your ambitions. Small people always do that, but the really great make you feel that you, too, can become great.

———

Don't part with your illusions. When they are gone, you may still exist, but you have ceased to live.

When a man goes back to look at the house of his childhood, it has always shrunk: there is no instance of such a house being as big as the picture in memory and imagination calls for.

Against a diseased imagination, demonstration goes for nothing.

On Laughter

Against the assault of laughter nothing can stand.

The human race has one really effective weapon, and that is laughter.

Comedy keeps the heart sweet.

———

Power, money, persuasion, supplication, persecution—these can lift at a colossal humbug—push it a little—weaken it a little over the course of a century; but only laughter can blow it to rags and atoms at a blast.

Laughter without a tinge of philosophy is but a sneeze of humor. Genuine humor is replete with wisdom.

Humor must be one of the chief attributes of God. Plants and animals that are distinctly humorous in form and characteristics are God's jokes.

Humor must not professedly teach and it must not professedly preach, but it must do both if it would live forever.

The best way to cheer yourself is to try to cheer somebody else up.

Are you so unobservant as not to have found out that sanity and happiness are an impossible combination?

Happiness is a Swedish sunset—it is there for all, but most of us look the other way and lose it.

On Life & Death

Let us endeavor so to live that when we come to die even the undertaker will be sorry.

Why is it that we rejoice at a birth and grieve at a funeral? It is because we are not the person involved.

When we remember we are all mad, the mysteries disappear and life stands explained.

Pity is for the living, envy is for the dead.

Each person is born to one possession which outvalues all his others—his last breath.

Death, the only immortal who treats us all alike, whose pity and whose peace and whose refuge are for all—the soiled and the pure, the rich and the poor, the loved and the unloved.

The first half of life consists of the capacity to enjoy without the chance; the last half consists of the chance without the capacity.

In time, the Deity perceived that death was a mistake—it allowed the dead person to escape from all further persecution in the blessed refuge of the grave. This was not satisfactory. A way must be contrived to pursue the dead beyond the tomb. . . . He invented Hell, and proclaimed it.

All say, "How hard it is to die"—a strange complaint to come from the mouths of people who have had to live.

As for me, I hope to be cremated. I made that remark to my pastor once, who said, with what he seemed to think was an impressive manner: "I wouldn't worry about that, if I had your chances."

I have a human distaste for death, as applied to myself, but I see nothing very solemn about it as applied to anybody.

There was never yet an uninteresting life. . . . Inside of the dullest exterior there is a drama, a comedy, and a tragedy.

The reports of my death are greatly exaggerated.

On Feelings of Loss

[On hearing of the death of his daughter, Suzy Clemens] It is one of the mysteries of our nature that a man, all unprepared, can receive a thunder-stroke like that and live. There is but one reasonable explanation of it. The intellect is stunned by the shock and but gropingly gathers the meaning of the words. The power to realize their full import is mercifully lacking.

Nothing that grieves us can be called little: by the eternal laws of proportion a child's loss of a doll and a king's loss of a crown are events of the same size.

The dreamer's valuation of a thing lost—not another man's—is the only standard to measure it by, and his grief for it makes it large and great and fine, and is worthy of our reverence in all cases.

On Love & Marriage

THE COURTSHIP

Courtship lifts a young fellow far and away above his common earthly self and by an impulse natural to those lofty regions he puts on his halo and his heavenly war paint and plays archangel as if he were born to it. He is working a deception, but is not aware of it.

When you fish for love, bait with your heart, not your brain.

Love is a madness; if thwarted it develops fast.

THE AFFECTION

Praise is well, compliment is well, but affection—that is the last and final and most precious reward that any man can win, whether by character or achievement.

THE INSTITUTION

Love seems the swiftest, but it is the slowest of all growths. No man or woman really knows what perfect love is until they have been married a quarter of a century.

People talk about the beautiful friendships between two persons of the same sex. What is the best of that sort, as compared with the friendship of man and wife, where the best impulses and highest ideals of both are the same? There is no place for comparison between the two friendships; the one is earthly, the other divine.

THE FIGHTING

A woman springs a sudden reproach upon you which provokes a hot retort—and then she will presently ask you to apologize.

You can't reason with your heart; it has its own laws, and thumps about things which the intellect scorns.

THE SHARING

Grief can take care of itself; but to get the full value of a joy you must have somebody to divide it with.

THE BUILDING

When we were finishing our house, we found we had a little cash left over, on account of the plumber not knowing it.

THE BABIES

Sufficient unto the day is one baby. As long as you are in your right mind don't you ever pray for twins. Twins amount to a permanent riot; and there ain't any real difference between triplets and a resurrection.

———

A baby is an inestimable blessing and bother.

A soiled baby with a neglected nose cannot be conscientiously regarded as a thing of beauty.

Adam and Eve had many advantages, but the principal one was that they escaped teething.

THE ANNIVERSARIES

What ought to be done to the man who invented the celebrating of anniversaries? Mere killing would be too light. Anniversaries are very well up to a certain point, while one's babies are in the process of growing up: they are joy-flags that make gay the road and prove progress; and one looks down the fluttering rank with pride. Then presently one notices that the flagstaffs are in process of a mysterious change of some sort—change of shape. Yes, they are turning into milestones. They are marking something lost now, not gained. From that time on it were best to suppress taking notice of anniversaries.

———

THE ROMANCE

To be human is to have one's little modicum of romance secreted away in one's composition. One never ceases to make a hero of one's self in private.

The romance of life is the only part of it which is overwhelmingly valuable, and romance dies with youth. After that, life is a drudge, & indeed a sham.

THE NEED

[Responding to "In a world without women what would men become?"] Scarce, sir. Mighty scarce.

After all these years, I see that I was mistaken about Eve in the beginning; it is better to live outside the Garden with her than inside it without her.

On Matters of Opinion

It were not best that we would all think alike; it is the difference of opinion that makes horse races.

I am not one of those who in expressing opinions confine themselves to facts.

If you cannot have a whale's good opinion except at some sacrifice of principle or personal dignity, it is better to try to live without it. That is my idea about whales.

Loyalty to petrified opinion never yet broke a chain or freed a human soul in this world—and never will.

We have two opinions: one private, which we are afraid to express; and another one—the one we use—which we force ourselves to wear . . . until habit makes us comfortable in it, and the custom of defending it presently makes us love it, adore it, and forget how pitifully we came by it.

We all know that in all matters of mere opinion that man is insane—just as insane as we are . . . we know exactly where to put our finger upon his insanity: it is where his opinion differs from ours. . . . All Democrats are insane, but not one of them knows it. None but the Republicans. All the Republicans are insane, but only the Democrats can perceive it. The rule is perfect: in all matters of opinion our adversaries are insane.

When we are young we generally estimate an opinion by the size of the person that holds it, but later we find that is an uncertain rule, for we realize that there are times when a hornet's opinion disturbs us more than an emperor's.

Sane and intelligent human beings are like all other human beings, and carefully and cautiously and diligently conceal their private real opinions from the world and give out fictitious ones in their stead for general consumption.

I, like all other human beings, expose to the world only my trimmed and perfumed and carefully barbered public opinions and conceal carefully, cautiously, wisely, my private ones.

Our opinions do not really blossom into fruition until we have expressed them to someone else.

Is a person's public and private opinion the same? It is thought there have been instances.

We are nothing but echoes. We have no thoughts of our own, no opinions of our own, we are but a compost heap made up of the decayed heredities, moral and physical.

Opinions based upon theory, superstition, and ignorance are not very precious.

In the matter of slavish imitation, man is the monkey's superior all the time. The average man is destitute of independence of opinion.

Its name is Public Opinion. It is held in reverence. It settles everything. Some think it is the voice of God.

In morals, conduct, and beliefs we take the color of our environment and associations, and it is a color that can be safely warranted to wash.

Whenever you find that you are on the side of the majority, it is time to reform.

Hain't we got all the fools in town on our side? And ain't that a big enough majority in any town?—*The Adventures of Huckleberry Finn* (1884)

ON MONEY

WANTING IT

What is the chief end of man?—to get rich. In what way?—dishonestly if he can; honestly if he must.

[Twain agrees with a friend's comment that the money of a certain industrialist is "tainted"] That's right. 'Taint yours, and 'taint mine.

To be satisfied with what one has; that is wealth. As long as one sorely needs a certain additional amount, that man isn't rich.

Few of us can stand prosperity. Another man's, I mean.

The lack of money is the root of all evil.

MAKING IT

All you need in this life is ignorance and confidence, and then success is sure.

Let your secret sympathies and your compassion be always with the underdog in the fight—this is magnanimity; but bet on the other one—this is business.

Honesty is the best policy—when there is money in it.

There are two times in a man's life when he should not speculate: when he can't afford it, and when he can.

WORKING FOR IT

Even Noah got no salary for the first six months—partly on account of the weather and partly because he was learning navigation.

No one with a specialty can hope to have a monopoly of it.

For business reasons, I must preserve the outward signs of sanity.

BORROWING IT

Scientists have odious manners, except when you prop up their theory; then you can borrow money off them.

—

Beautiful credit! The foundation of modern society.

[Letter sent by Twain to Andrew Carnegie]
Dear Sir and Friend,

> You seem to be in prosperity. Could you lend an admirer $1.50 to buy a hymn-book with? I will bless you. God will bless you—I feel it; I know it—and it will do a great deal of good.

Yours Truly,
Mark Twain

P.S. Don't send the hymn-book; send the money; I want to make the selection myself.

LENDING IT

A banker is a person who lends you his umbrella when the sun is shining and wants it back the minute it rains.

One must keep one's character. Earn a character first if you can, and if you can't, then assume one. From the code of morals I have been following and revising and revising for 72 years I remember one detail. All my life I have been honest—comparatively honest. I could

never use money I had not made honestly—I could
only lend it.

DONATING IT
Remember the poor—it costs nothing.

SPENDING IT
I wonder how much it would take to buy a soap-
bubble, if there was only one in the world.

A man pretty much always refuses another man's first
offer, no matter what it is.

It is no use to throw a good thing away merely because
the market isn't ripe yet.

FILING SUIT FOR IT
I can't do literary work the rest of this year because I'm
meditating another law suit and looking around for a
defendant.

I have seen an entire family lifted out of poverty and
into affluence by the simple boon of a broken leg. I
have had people come to me on crutches, with tears in

their eyes, to bless this beneficent institution. In all my experiences of life, I have seen nothing so seraphic as the look that comes into a freshly mutilated man's face when he feels in his vest pocket with his remaining hand and finds his accident ticket all right.

AND, ALWAYS, REVERING IT

Some men worship rank, some worship heroes, some worship God, and over these ideals they dispute—but they all worship money.

Make money and the whole world will conspire to call you a gentleman.

Virtue has never been as respectable as money.

Prosperity is the best protector of principle.

ON POLITICS

POLITICS IN GENERAL

In religion and politics people's beliefs and convictions are in almost every case gotten at second-hand, and without examination, from authorities who have not themselves examined the questions at issue but have taken them at second-hand from other non-examiners, whose opinions about them were not worth a brass farthing.

[On the recent death of a politician] I did not attend his funeral; but I wrote a nice letter saying I approved of it.

The radical invents the views. When he has worn them out, the conservative adopts them.

I am a revolutionist by birth, reading and principle. I am always on the side of the revolutionists because there was never a revolution unless there were some oppressive and intolerable conditions against which to revolute.

An honest man in politics shines more than he would elsewhere.

Strip the human race absolutely naked and it would be a real democracy.

In statesmanship get the formalities right, never mind about the moralities.

The principle of give and take is the principle of diplomacy—give one and take ten.

By and by when each nation has 2,000 battleships and 5,000,000 soldiers we shall all be safe and the wisdom of statesmanship will stand confirmed.

They want to send me abroad, as a Consul or a Minister. I said I didn't want any of the pie. God knows I am mean enough and lazy enough, now, without being a foreign consul.

AND CONGRESS IN PARTICULAR
It could probably be shown by facts and figures that there is no distinctly native American criminal class except Congress.

A flea can be taught everything a congressman can.

Suppose you were an idiot, and suppose you were a member of Congress, but I repeat myself.

Public servants: Persons chosen by the people to distribute the graft.

ON OUR RIGHTS INALIENABLE

It is by the goodness of God that in our country we have those three unspeakably precious things; freedom of speech, freedom of conscience, and the prudence never to practice either of them.

There isn't a Parallel of Latitude but thinks it would have been the Equator if it had had its rights.

Man has not a single right which is the product of anything but might. Not a single right is indestructible: a new might can at any time abolish it, hence, man possesses not a single permanent right.

Whose property is my body? Probably mine. I so regard it. If I experiment with it, who must be answerable? I, not the state. If I choose injudiciously, does the state die? Oh, no.

IMPERIALISM INTOLERABLE

The political and commercial morals of the United States are not merely food for laughter, they are an entire banquet.

Enlarging his sphere of influence. That is a courteous modern phrase which means robbing your neighbor—for your neighbor's benefit.

Man is the only animal that robs his helpless fellow of his country—takes possession of it and drives him out of it or destroys him. Man has done this in all the ages. There is not an acre of ground on the globe that is in possession of its rightful owner, or that has not been taken away from owner after owner, cycle after cycle, by force and bloodshed.

In a sordid slime harmonious,
Greed was born in yonder ditch,
With a longing in his bosom—and for others'
goods an itch—
As Christ died to make men holy, let
men die to make us rich—
Our god is marching on.

[to the tune of "The Battle Hymn of the
Republic"]

Two or three centuries from now it will be recognized
that all the competent killers are Christians; then the
pagan world will go to school to the Christian—not to
acquire his religion, but his guns.

Extending the Blessings of Civilization to our Brother
who Sits in Darkness has been a good trade and has
paid well, on the whole; and there is money in it yet, if
carefully worked—but not enough, in my judgment, to
make any considerable risk advisable.

"Our Country, right or wrong . . ." Have you not perceived that the phrase is an insult to the nation? . . . Only when a republic's life is in danger should a man uphold his government when it is in the wrong. There is no other time. The republic's life is not in peril.

Where every man in a state has a vote, brutal laws are impossible.

No country can be well governed unless its citizens as a body keep religiously before their minds that they are the guardians of the law, and that the law officers are only the machinery for its execution, nothing more.

ON PREJUDICE

The very ink with which history is written is merely fluid prejudice.

Where prejudice exists it always discolors our thoughts.

I have no color prejudices nor caste prejudices nor creed prejudices. All I care to know is that a man is a human being, and that is enough for me; he can't be any worse.

We are chameleons, and our partialities and prejudices change with place with an easy and blessed facility.

On Religion

Man is a Religious Animal. He is the only Religious Animal. He is the only animal that has the True Religion—several of them.

Religion consists in a set of things which the average man thinks he believes and wishes he was certain.

It is agreed, in this country, that if a man can arrange his religion so that it perfectly satisfies his conscience, it is not incumbent on him to care whether the arrangement is satisfactory to anyone else or not.

I admire the serene assurance of those who have religious faith. It is wonderful to observe the calm confidence of a Christian with four aces.

Church ain't shucks to a circus.

If Christ were here now there is one thing he would not be—a Christian.

Martyrdom covers a multitude of sins.

The Church is always trying to get other people to reform; it might not be a bad idea to reform itself a little by way of example.

A man is accepted into a church for what he believes and he is turned out for what he knows.

Tom [Sawyer] turned in without the added vexation of prayers.

One of the proofs of the immortality of the soul is that myriads have believed in it. They have also believed the world was flat.

We have infinite trouble in solving man-made mysteries; it is only when we set out to discover the secrets of God that our difficulties disappear.

The Christian's Bible is a drug store. Its contents remain the same, but the medical practice changes.

Most people are bothered by those passages in Scripture which they cannot understand; but as for me, I always noticed that the passages in Scripture which trouble me most are those that I do understand.

The Bible has noble poetry in it; and some clever fables; and some blood drenched history; and a wealth of obscenity; and upwards of a thousand lies.

Providence protects children and idiots. I know because I have tested it.

There are many scapegoats for our blunders, but the most popular one is Providence.

I never did a thing in all my life, virtuous or otherwise that I didn't repent of within twenty-four hours.

There is nothing more awe-inspiring than a miracle except the credulity that can take it at par.

On Revenge

There is more real pleasure to be gotten out of a malicious act, where your heart is in it, than out of thirty acts of a nobler sort.

Therein lies the defect of revenge: it's all in the anticipation; the thing itself is a pain, not a pleasure; at least the pain is the biggest end of it.

On Science & Stars

There is something fascinating about science. One gets such wholesale returns of conjecture out of such a trifling investment of fact.

There ain't no way to find out why a snorer can't hear himself snore.

Name the greatest of all inventors: ACCIDENT.

I do not see how astronomers can help feeling exquisitely insignificant, for every new page of the Book of the Heavens they open reveals to them more and more that the world we are so proud of is to the universe of careening globes as is one mosquito to the winged and hoofed flocks and herds that darken the air and populate the plains and forests of all the earth. If you killed the mosquito would it be missed? Verily, What is Man, that he should be considered of God?

An occultation of Venus is not half so difficult as an eclipse of the sun, but because it comes seldom the world thinks it's a grand thing.

Constellations have always been troublesome things to name. If you give one of them a fanciful name, it will always refuse to live up to it; it will always persist in not resembling the thing it has been named for.

If I were going to construct a God I would furnish Him with some ways and qualities and characteristics which the Present One lacks. . . . He would spend some of His eternities in trying to forgive Himself for making man unhappy when He could have made him happy with the same effort and He would spend the rest of them in studying astronomy.

ON SELF-APPROVAL OR
THE LACK OF IT

From his cradle to his grave man never does a single thing which has any first and foremost objective save one—to secure peace of mind, spiritual comfort, for himself.

What do you call Love, Hate, Charity, Revenge, Humanity, Magnanimity, Forgiveness? Different results of the one Master Impulse: the necessity of securing one's self-approval.

When people do not respect us we are sharply offended; yet deep down in his heart no man much respects himself.

It may be called the Master Passion, the hunger for self-approval.

A man cannot be comfortable without his own approval.

If everybody was satisfied with himself there would be no heroes.

On a Very Private Matter of Sin

Of all the kinds of sexual intercourse, this has least to recommend it. As an amusement it is too fleeting, as an occupation it is too wearing; as a public exhibition there is no money in it. It has, in our last day of progress and improvement, been degraded to brotherhood with flat-ulence—among the best bred these two arts are now in-dulged only in private—though by consent of the whole company, when only males are present, it is still permissible, in good society, to remove the embargo upon the fundamental sigh.

Caesar in his *Commentaries,* says, to the lonely it is company; to the forsaken it is a friend; to the aged and impotent it is a benefactor; they that be penniless are yet rich, in that they still have this majestic diversion. There are times when I prefer it to sodomy.

The monkey is the only animal, except man, that practices this science; hence he is our brother; there is a bond of sympathy and relationship between us. Give this ingenious animal an audience of the proper kind, and he will straightway put aside his other affairs and take a whet; and you will see by the contortions and his ecstatic expression that he takes an intelligent and human interest in his performance.

To a man all things are possible but one—he cannot have a hole in the seat of his breeches and keep his fingers out of it. A man does seem to feel more distress and more persistent and distracting solicitude about such a thing than he could about a sick child that was threatening to grow worse every time he took his attention away from it.

On "Sivilization"

The Widow Douglas, she took me for her son, and allowed she would sivilize me; but it was rough living in the house all the time, considering how dismal regular and decent the widow was in all her ways; and so when I couldn't stand it no longer, I lit out. I got into my old rags, and my sugar-hogshead again, and was free and satisfied. But Tom Sawyer, he hunted me up and said he was going to start a band of robbers, and I might join if I would go back to the widow and be respectable. So I went back.—*Adventures of Huckleberry Finn* (1884)

Civilization: A limitless multiplication of unnecessary necessities.

All the modern inconveniences.

Is there no salvation for us but to adopt Civilization and lift ourselves down to its level?

The first thing a missionary teaches a savage is indecency.

Soap and education are not as sudden as a massacre but they are more deadly in the long run.

We white people are merely modified Thugs; Thugs fretting under the restraints of a not very thick skin of civilization. . . .

He was a gentleman all over; and so was his family. He was well-born, as the saying is, and that's worth as much in a man as it is in a horse.

On Sports

Baseball is the very symbol of the outward and visible expression of the drive and push and rush and struggle of the raging, tearing, booming nineteenth century.

Golf is a good walk spoiled.

Do not tell fish stories where the people know you; but particularly, don't tell them where they know the fish.

Get a bicycle. You will not regret it. If you live.

On Storytelling

I like a good story well told. That's the reason I am sometimes forced to tell them myself.

If you wish to lower yourself in a person's favor, one good way is to tell his story over again, the way *you* heard it.

There are few stories that have anything superlatively good in them except the *idea*—and that is always bettered by transplanting.

People who early learn the right way to choose a dentist have their reward. . . . All dentists talk while they work. They have inherited this from their professional ancestors, the barbers. The dentist who talks well— other things being equal—is the one to choose.

The humorous story is told gravely; the teller does his best to conceal the fact that he even dimly suspects that there is anything funny about it.

The humorous story is American, the comic story is English, the witty story is French. The humorous story depends for its effect upon the *manner* of the telling; the comic story and the witty story upon the *matter*.

The humorist writer professes to awaken and direct your love, your pity, your kindness—your scorn for untruth, pretension, imposture. . . . He takes upon himself to be the week-day preacher.

Repetition is a mighty power in the domain of humor. If frequently used, nearly any precisely worded and unchanging formula will eventually compel laughter if it be gravely and earnestly repeated, at intervals, five or six times.

To string incongruities and absurdities together in a wandering and sometimes purposeless way, and seem innocently unaware that they are absurdities, is the basis of the American art. . . . Another feature is the slurring of the point. A third is the dropping of a studied remark apparently without knowing it, as if one were thinking aloud. The fourth and last is the pause.

On the Commandments

It is not best that we use our morals weekdays; it gets them out of repair for Sundays.

ADULTERY

"Thou shalt not commit adultery" is a command which makes no distinction between the following persons. They are all required to obey it: children at birth. Children in the cradle. School children. Youths and maidens. Fresh adults. Older ones. Men and women of 40. Of 50. Of 60. Of 70. Of 80. Of 90. Of 100. The command does not distribute its burden equally, and cannot. It is not hard upon the three sets of children.

Familiarity breeds contempt—and children.

KILLING

If the desire to kill and the opportunity to kill came always together, who would escape hanging?

We have an insanity plea that would have saved Cain.

BLASPHEMY

Under certain circumstances, urgent circumstances, desperate circumstances, profanity provides a relief denied even to prayer.

He began with that word "H." That's a long word and a profane word. I don't remember what the word was now, but I recognized the power of it. I had never used that language myself, but at that moment I was converted. It has been a great refuge for me in time of trouble. If a man doesn't know that language he can't express himself on strenuous occasions. When you have that word at your command let trouble come.

A man's character may be learned from the adjectives which he habitually uses in conversation.

I was . . . blaspheming my luck in a way that made my breath smell of brimstone.

The idea that no gentleman ever swears is all wrong. He can swear and still be a gentleman if he does it in a nice and benevolent and affectionate way.

When angry count four; when very angry, swear.

Her eyes blazed up, and she jumped for him like a wild-cat, and when she was done with him she was rags and he wasn't anything but an allegory.

There ought to be a room in every house to swear in. It's dangerous to have to repress an emotion like that.

He didn't utter a word, but he exuded mute blasphemy from every pore.

The spirit of wrath—and not the words—is the sin; and the spirit of wrath is cursing. We begin to swear before we can talk.

I sent down . . . and hired an artist by the week to sit up nights and curse that stranger, and give me a lift occasionally in the daytime when I came to a hard place.

When it comes down to pure ornamental cursing, the native American is gifted above the sons of men.

All through the first ten years of my married life I kept a constant and discreet watch upon my tongue while in the house, and went outside and to a distance when circumstances were too much for me and I was obliged to seek relief. I prized my wife's respect and approval above all the rest of the human race's respect and approval. I dreaded the day when she should discover that I was but a whited sepulcher partly freighted with suppressed language. I was so careful, during ten years, that

I had not a doubt that my suppressions had been successful. Therefore I was quite as happy in my guilt as I could have been if I had been innocent.

I have some new sleeve buttons . . . beautiful anticussers. You can put them in and take them out without a change of temper. . . .

My swearing doesn't mean any more to me than your sermons do to you.

If I cannot swear in heaven I shall not stay there.

STEALING

Nothing incites to money-crimes like great poverty or great wealth.

A robber is much more high-toned than what a pirate is—as a general thing. In most countries they're awful high up in the nobility—dukes and such.

Really, what we want now, is not laws against crime, but a law against insanity. That is where the true evil lies.

As by the fires of experience, so by commission of crime you learn real morals. Commit all crimes, familiarize yourself with all sins, take them in rotation (there are only two or three thousand of them), stick to it, commit two or three every day, and by and by you will be proof against them. When you are through you will be proof against all sins and morally perfect. You will be vaccinated against every possible commission of them. This is the only way.

ON THE MERITS OF ALCOHOLIC SPIRITS

What marriage is to morality, a properly conducted licensed liquor traffic is to sobriety.

Intemperate temperance injures the cause of temperance, while temperate temperance helps it in its fight against intemperate intemperance.

Of the demonstrably wise there are but two: those who commit suicide, and those who keep their reasoning faculties atrophied with drink.

I prefer milk because I am a Prohibitionist, but I do not go to it for inspiration.

Scotch whisky . . . I always take it at night as a preventive of toothache. I have never had the toothache; and what is more, I never intend to have it.

ON THE ARTS

ON CLASSICAL MUSIC

I have never heard enough classical music to be able to enjoy it; and the simple truth is, I detest it. Not mildly, but with all my heart . . . partly because of the nights of suffering I have endured in its presence, and partly because I want to love it and can't. I suppose one naturally hates the things he wants to love and can't.

When you want genuine music—music that will come right home to you like a bad quarter, suffuse your system like strychnine whisky, go right through you like Brandreth's pills, ramify your whole constitution like the measles, and break out on your hide like the pinfeather pimples on a picked goose—when you want all this, just smash your piano, and invoke the glory-beaming banjo!

THE OPERA

In America the opera is an affectation. The seeming love for [it] is a lie.

One in fifty of those who attend our operas like it already, perhaps, but I think a good many of the other forty-nine go in order to learn to like it, and the rest in order to be able to talk knowingly about it. The latter usually hum the airs while they are being sung, so that their neighbors may perceive that they have been to operas before. The funeral of these do not occur often enough.

I have attended operas, whenever I could not help it. . . .

I am sure I know of no agony comparable to the listening to an unfamiliar opera.

I have been told that Wagner's music is better than it sounds.

I have witnessed and greatly enjoyed the first act of everything which Wagner created, but the effect on me has always been so powerful that one act was quite sufficient; whenever I have witnessed two acts I have gone away physically exhausted; and whenever I have ventured an entire opera the result has been the next thing to suicide.

There isn't often anything in Wagner opera that one would call by such a violent name as acting; as a rule all you would see would be a couple of . . . people, one of them standing, the other catching flies. Of course I do not really mean that he would be catching flies; I only mean that the usual operatic gestures which consist in reaching first one hand out into the air then the other might suggest the sport I speak of if the operator attended strictly to business. . . .

The banging and slamming and booming and crashing [in *Lohengrin*] were something beyond belief. The racking and pitiless pain of it remains stored up in my memory alongside the memory of the time that I had my teeth fixed. . . .

There is where the deep ingenuity of the operatic idea is betrayed. It deals so largely in pain that its scattered delights are prodigiously augmented by the contrasts.

I was not able to detect in the vocal parts of *Parsifal* anything that might with confidence be called rhythm or tune or melody; one person performed at a time—and a long time, too—often in a noble, and always in a high-toned, voice; but he only pulled out long notes, then some short ones, then another long one, then a sharp, quick, peremptory bark or two—and so on and so on; and when he was done you saw that the information which he had conveyed had not compensated for the disturbance.

ON PHOTOGRAPHY

A photograph is a most important document, and there is nothing more damning to go down to posterity than a silly, foolish smile caught and fixed forever.

The sun never looks through the photographic instrument that it does not print a lie.

The piece of glass it prints it on is well named a "negative"—a contradiction—a misrepresentation—a falsehood. I speak feeling of this matter, because by turns the instrument has represented me to be a lunatic, a Solomon, a missionary, a burglar and an abject idiot, and I am neither.

PAINTING AND SCULPTURE

I'm glad the old masters are all dead, and I only wish they had died sooner.

Can it be possible that the painters make John the Baptist a Spaniard in Madrid and an Irishman in Dublin?

A good legible label is usually worth, for information, a ton of significant attitude and expression in a historical picture.

[On Joseph Mallord William Turner's *The Slave Ship*] A tortoise-shell cat having a fit in a platter of tomatoes . . .

Even popularity can be overdone. In Rome, along at first, you are full of regrets that Michaelangelo died; but by and by you only regret that you didn't see him do it.

[On a Phidias sculpture] It looked natural because it looked somehow as if it were in pain.

Criticism is a queer thing. If I print, "She was stark naked" and then proceeded to describe her person in detail, what critic would not howl? Who would venture to leave the book on a parlor table? But the artist does this and all ages gather around and look and talk and point.

Architects cannot teach nature anything.

ON THE BASICS OF WRITING

GOOD WRITING IS CRAFTSMANSHIP
Training is everything. The peach was once a bitter almond; cauliflower is nothing but cabbage with a college education.

It usually takes me more than three weeks to prepare a good impromptu speech.

If you invent two or three people and turn them loose in your manuscript, something is bound to happen to them—you can't help it; and then it will take you the rest of the book to get them out of the natural consequences of that occurrence, and so first thing you know, there's your book all finished up and never cost you an idea.

IT IS CRAFTY WITH TRUTH

Most writers regard the truth as their most valuable possession, and therefore are most economical in its use.

Delicacy—a sad, sad false delicacy—robs literature of the two best things among its belongings: Family-circle narratives and obscene stories.

I don't know anything that mars good literature so completely as too much truth.

BUT, REGRETTABLY, NOT WITH SPELLING

Why, there isn't a man who doesn't have to throw out about fifteen hundred words a day when he writes his letters because he can't spell them! It's like trying to do a St. Vitus dance with wooden legs.

I have had an aversion to good spelling for sixty years and more, merely for the reason that when I was a boy there was not a thing I could do creditably except spell according to the book. It was a poor and mean distinction and I early learned to disenjoy it. I suppose that this is because the ability to spell correctly is a talent, not an acquirement. There is some dignity about an acquirement, because it is a product of your own labor. It is wages earned, whereas to be able to do a thing merely by the grace of God and not by your own effort transfers the distinction to our heavenly home—where possibly it is a matter of pride and satisfaction but it leaves you naked and bankrupt.

I never had any large respect for good spelling. That is my feeling yet. Before the spelling-book came with its arbitrary forms, men unconsciously revealed shades of their characters and also added enlightening shades of expression to what they wrote by their spelling, and so it is possible that the spelling-book has been a doubtful benevolence to us.

Simplified spelling is all right, but, like chastity, you can carry it too far.

Ours is a mongrel language which started with a child's vocabulary of three hundred words, and now consists of two hundred and twenty-five thousand; the whole lot, with the exception of the original and legitimate three hundred, borrowed, stolen, smouched from every unwatched language under the sun, the spelling of each individual word of the lot locating the source of the theft and preserving the memory of the revered crime.

BAD WRITING CAN BE PROSE

What a lumbering poor vehicle prose is for the conveying of a great thought! . . . Prose wanders around with a lantern and laboriously schedules and verifies the details and particulars of a valley and its frame of crags and peaks, then Poetry comes, and lays bare the whole landscape with a single splendid flash.

As to the adjective: when in doubt, strike it out.

OR IN PUN

No circumstances, however dismal, will ever be considered a sufficient excuse for the admission of that last and saddest evidence of intellectual poverty, the Pun.

Since England and America have been joined in Kipling, may they not be severed in Twain.

AND STILL, OFTEN, BE "CLASSIC"
A "Classic." Something that everyone wants to have read and nobody wants to read.

And as for the *Bostonians,* I would rather be damned to John Bunyan's heaven than read that.

[On Shakespeare] Why it ain't *human* talk; nobody that ever lived, ever talked the way they do. Even the flunkies can't say the simplest thing the way a human being would say it. "Me lord hath given command-ment, sirrah, that the vehicle wherein he doth of an-cient custom, his daily recreation take, shall unto the portal of the palace be straight conveyed; the which commandment, mark ye well, admitteth not of waste-ful dalliance, like to the tranquil mark of yon gilded moon athwart the dappled fields of space, but, even as the molten meteor cleaves the skies, or the red-tongued bolts of heaven, charged with death, to their dread office speed, let this, me lord's commandment, have instant consummation!"

Pilgrim's Progress, about a man that left his family, it didn't say why.

My works are like water. The works of the great masters are like wine. But everyone drinks water.

Creed and opinion change with time, and their symbols perish; but literature and its temples are sacred to all creeds and inviolate.

ON EDITORS

How often we recall, with regret, that Napoleon once shot at a magazine editor and missed him and killed a publisher. But we remember with charity, that his intentions were good.

Only kings, editors and people with tapeworm have the right to use the editorial "we."

It is discouraging to try to penetrate a mind like yours. You ought to get it out and dance on it. That would take some of the rigidity out of it. . . . You really must get your mind out and have it repaired; you see, yourself, that it is all caked together.
[letter to a man who edited his introduction to *The Personal Recollections of Joan of Arc* (1896)]

AND PUBLISHERS

All publishers are Columbuses. The successful author is their America. The reflection that they—like Columbus—didn't discover what they expected to discover, and didn't discover what they started out to discover, doesn't trouble them. All they remember is that they discovered America; they forget that they started out to discover some patch or corner of India.

Robbery of a publisher—I said that if he regarded that as a crime it was because his education was limited.

I said it was not a crime and was always rewarded in heaven with two haloes. Would be, if it ever happened.

They always talk handsomely about the literature of the land. . . . And in the midst of their enthusiasm they turn around to do what they can to discourage it.

Whenever a copyright law is to be made or altered, then the idiots assemble.

Only one thing is impossible for God: to find any sense in any copyright law on the planet.

ON THE DAMNED HUMAN RACE

Man is the only animal that blushes. Or needs to.

The fact that man knows right from wrong proves his *intellectual* superiority to the other creatures; but the fact that he can *do* wrong proves his *moral* inferiority to any creature that *cannot*.

As a thinker and planner the ant is the equal of any savage race of men; as a self-educated specialist in several arts she is the superior of any savage race of men; and in one or two high mental qualities she is above the reach of any man, savage or civilized.

Of all the animals, man is the only one that is cruel. He is the only one that inflicts pain for the pleasure of doing it.

If you pick up a starving dog and make him prosperous, he will not bite you. This is the principal difference between a dog and a man.

It is just like man's vanity and impertinence to call an animal dumb because it is dumb to his dull perceptions.

If a man could be crossed with a cat, it would improve man, but it would deteriorate the cat.

The human race consists of the dangerously insane and such as are not.

By trying we can easily learn to endure adversity. Another man's, I mean.

Everything human is pathetic. The secret source of Humor itself is not joy but sorrow. There is not humor in heaven.

Man is without any doubt the most interesting fool there is. Also the most eccentric. He hasn't a single written law, in his Bible or out of it, which has any but one purpose and intention—to limit or defeat a law of God.

Man the machine—man the impersonal engine. Whatsoever a man is, is due to his make, and to the influence brought to bear upon it by his heredities, his habitat, his associations. He is moved, corrected, COMMANDED, by exterior influences—solely. He originates nothing, not even a thought.

There are times when one would like to hang the whole human race, and finish the farce.

Human nature is the same everywhere; it deifies success, it has nothing but scorn for defeat.

Every one is a moon, and has a dark side which he never shows to anybody.

What is the most rigorous law of our being? Growth. No smallest atom of our moral, mental, or physical structure can stand still a year. It grows—it must grow; nothing can prevent it.

Man will do many things to get himself loved; he will do all things to get himself envied.

We all do no end of feeling, and we mistake it for thinking.

There is no character, howsoever good and fine, but it can be destroyed by ridicule, howsoever poor and witless. Observe the ass, for instance: his character is about perfect, he is the choicest spirit among all the humbler animals, yet see what ridicule has brought him to. Instead of feeling complimented when we are called an ass, we are left in doubt.

One must keep one's character. Earn a character first if you can, and if you can't, then assume one.

It is not worth while to try to keep history from repeating itself, for man's character will always make the preventing of the repetitions impossible.

There is a breed of humility which is *itself* a species of showing off.

HABIT/VICE

To promise not to do a thing is the surest way in the world to make a body want to go and do that very thing.

Habit is habit, and not to be flung out of the window by any man, but coaxed downstairs a step at a time.

It is easier to get out than stay out.

Nothing so needs reforming as other people's habits.

A man may have no bad habits and have worse.

COWARDICE

The human race is a race of cowards; and I am not only marching in that procession but carrying a banner.

Courage is resistance to fear, mastery of fear—not absence of fear.

———

There are several good protections against temptation, but the surest is cowardice.

We all live in the protection of certain cowardices which we call our principles.

ENVY

Envy . . . the only thing which men will sell both body and soul to get.

ON THE POWER OF THE PRESS

The New York papers have long known that no large question is ever really settled until I have been consulted.

There are only two forces that can carry light to all corners of the globe—the sun in the heavens and the Associated Press.

———

Many a small thing has been made large by the right kind of advertising.

As for myself, I have no difficulty in believing that our newspapers will by and by contain news, not twenty-four hours old from Jupiter et al—mainly astronomical corrections and weather indications; with now and then a sarcastic fling at the only true religion.

We have a criminal jury system which is superior to any in the world; and its efficiency is only marred by the difficulty of finding twelve men every day who don't know anything and can't read.

ON TRAVEL ABROAD

Travel is fatal to prejudice.

To forget pain is to be painless; to forget care is to be rid of it; to go abroad is to accomplish both.

A round man cannot be expected to fit in a square hole right away. He must have time to modify his shape.

ABROAD IN GERMANY

Whenever the literary German dives into a sentence, that is the last you are going to see of him till he emerges on the other side of the Atlantic with his verb in his mouth.

The Germans are exceedingly fond of Rhine wines. One tells them from the vinegar by the label.

A verb has a hard enough time of it in this world when it's all together. It's downright inhuman to split it up. But that's just what those Germans do. They take part of a verb and put it down here, like a stake, and they take the other part of it and put it away over yonder like another stake, and between those two limits they just shovel in German.

I was trying to explain to St. Peter, and was doing it in the German tongue, because I didn't want to be too explicit.

Germany, the diseased world's bathhouse.

ABROAD IN ENGLAND
I would like to live in Manchester, England. The transition between Manchester and death would be unnoticeable.

ABROAD IN ITALY
They spell it Vinci and pronounce it Vinchy; foreigners always spell better than they pronounce.

ABROAD IN SWITZERLAND
Switzerland is simply a large, humpy, solid rock, with a thin skin of grass stretched over it.

AND ABROAD IN FRANCE
In Marseilles they make half the toilet soap we consume in America, but the Marseillaise only have a vague theoretical idea of its use, which they have obtained from books of travel.

[How Twain felt while in Europe] As out of place as a Presbyterian in Hell.

O N   T R U T H   &   D A R N   G O O D   L I E S

Some people lie when they tell the truth. I tell the truth lying.

The history of the race, and each individual's experience, are thick with evidence that a truth is not hard to kill and that a lie told well is immortal.

When in doubt, tell the truth.

Why shouldn't truth be stranger than fiction? Fiction is obliged to stick to possibilities. Truth isn't.

One of the most striking differences between a cat and a lie is that a cat has only nine lives.

Carlyle said, "A lie cannot live"; it shows he did not know how to tell them.

There are three kinds of lies: lies, damned lies, and statistics.

Get your facts first, then you can distort them as you please.

Tell the truth or trump—but get the trick.

Why will you humbug yourselves with that foolish notion that no lie is a lie except a spoken one?

If you tell the truth you don't have to remember anything.

Barring that natural expression of villainy which we all have, the man looked honest enough.

Honesty: the best of all the lost arts.

There is only one way to find out if a man's honest: ask him, if he says yes, you know he is crooked.

People ought to start dead and then they would be honest so much earlier.

A historian who would convey the truth has got to lie. Often he must enlarge the truth by diameters, otherwise his reader would not be able to see it.

Many when they come to die have spent all the truth that was in them, and enter the next world as paupers. I have saved up enough to make an astonishment there.

ON WAR & PEACE

Peace by persuasion has a pleasant sound, but I think we should not be able to work it. We should have to tame the human race first, and history seems to show that that cannot be done.

The higher animals engage in individual fights, but never in organized masses. Man is the only animal that deals in the atrocity of atrocities. War.

The pitifulest thing out is a mob; that's what an army is—a mob; they don't fight with courage that's born in them, but with courage that's borrowed from their mass, and from their officers. But a mob without any man at the head of it, is beneath pitifulness.

THE WAR PRAYER

O Lord our Father, our young patriots, idols of our hearts, go forth to battle—be thou near them! . . . O Lord our God, help us to tear their soldiers to bloody shreds with our shells; help us to cover their smiling fields with the pale forms of their patriot dead: help us to drown the thunder of their guns with the shrieks of their wounded, writhing in pain; help us to lay waste their humble homes with a hurricane of fire; help us to wring the hearts of their unoffending widows with unavailing grief. . . . For our sakes who adore Thee, Lord, blast their hopes, blight their lives, protract their bitter pilgrimage, make heavy their steps, water their way with their tears, stain the white snow with the blood of their wounded feet! We ask it in the spirit of love, of Him who is the Source of Love, and who is the ever faithful refuge and friend of all who are sore beset and seek His aid with humble and contrite hearts.—*dictated c. 1904*

On Work & Play

Work consists of whatever a body is obliged to do, and play consists of whatever a body is not obliged to do.

Work and play are words used to describe the same thing under differing conditions.

I do not like work even when someone else does it.

Make it a point to do something every day that you don't want to do. This is the golden rule for acquiring the habit of doing your duty without pain.

To be busy is man's only happiness.

Do not put off until tomorrow what can be put off till day-after-tomorrow just as well.

Let us save tomorrows for work.

Sam Clemens never finished what he started—before the age of twenty-five, that is. By age twenty-five he had quit school to work for a newspaper typesetter, quit setting type to pilot a Mississippi steamer, quit river-boating to join the Confederate Army and, shortly thereafter, deserted the army to go West and dig for riches. Thankfully for generations of readers, he found none; and, while recouping his losses, he instead latched onto a bit of wisdom that would change the landscape of American literature.

"There comes a time in every rightly constructed boy's life that he has a raging desire to go somewhere and dig for hidden treasure."

And with that seemingly simple mix of insight, adolescence, irreverence and logic, the rambunctious outcast put on a white serge suit, picked up a pen, and reinvented himself. He chose as his nom de plume the call made on the Mississippi to sound the river shallows (mark twain!—literally, two fathoms). Giving free reign to his evolving opinions and prejudices, he became the world's most loved observer of human nature and sudden turns of fate.

Mark Twain was born Samuel Langhorne Clemens in Florida, Missouri, on 30 November 1835. As he later said, he was brought in on Halley's Comet and wished to go out on its return. He was raised in Hannibal, on the Missouri banks of the Mississippi. He was the sixth of seven children. At age twelve, sometime after his father's death in 1847, he left school and apprenticed at a local printer's shop. There, in what Abraham Lincoln later called the "poor boy's college," Clemens trained as a writer and critic.

> *"One isn't a printer ten years without setting up acres of good and bad literature, and learning— unconsciously at first, consciously later—to discriminate between the two . . . and meantime, he is unconsciously acquiring what is a 'style.'"*

The literature he set into type varied in genre from anecdotes, to monologues, brief book excerpts, poems, and sketches by contemporary humorists. What these selections had in common was that they were all self-contained pieces—short and to the point. "Training is," as Twain later wrote, "everything"; and so, it should come as no surprise that Twain himself survives in our hearts (and on the tip of our tongues) as easily excerptable and eminently quotable. We can all picture Tom Sawyer persuading his friends to pay money for the privilege to whitewash his fence, but how many of us remember the novel at length? That scene—rather than the plot—stays fresh in our minds because it encapsulates how much we admired and resented that conniving kid on our own block, or in the cubicle just outside our office door.

Twain would write short pieces for nearly two decades before penning his first novel. But it was his skills as a printer, and not a writer, that bought him his first ticket out of Hannibal. Working as a tramp printer, he traveled to St. Louis and Iowa and then east to New York, Philadelphia, and Washington, D.C. During that time, he contributed travel letters to his brother's newspaper, the *Hannibal Gazette*. A prolific writer, his career as a journalist was off to a fine start, writing feature stories, political reports, and sketches. Then, in 1857,

Twain traveled to New Orleans and apprenticed to the pilot master George Ealer on the steamboat *Pennsylvania*. One and a half years later, he was a licensed steamboat pilot.

By 1861, the Civil War had all but cut off traffic on the Mississippi. Twain enlisted in a Confederate company from Missouri. A few weeks later, he deserted and went off with his brother for the New Territory of Nevada. After failing as prospector, Twain served as city editor for the *Virginia City Enterprise*. One year later, in 1865, a real good liar and a jumping frog brought Twain into national prominence. New York's *The Saturday Press* published his "Celebrated Jumping Frog of Calaveras County," and newspapers throughout the United States reprinted it. In 1867, that jumping frog was binded with other short sketches by Twain as his first book.

In the meantime, as early as 1866, Twain began lecturing. He told stories about himself and about his travels, which he continued to make as a correspondent. Twain visited the Sandwich Islands and, in 1867, set sail for the Holy Land. Later, he toured France and Italy gathering material for *The Innocents Abroad*. This book, published in 1869, truly established Twain's reputation as a humorist. In it he satirized American tourists learning about Europe from guidebooks and, relying on his own voice of brash practicality, managed to extol the virtues of the New World as opposed to the Old.

After returning from Europe, Twain settled in Buffalo, New York, and worked as editor of a local newspaper. He met and married Olivia (Livy) Landon, the wealthy daughter of a New York coal merchant. The couple moved to Hartford, Connecticut, where they built a respectable home at the center of an artists' colony known as Nook Farm. Twain joined a publishing firm that failed. He made bad investments in new technology. And he recouped his losses lecturing and writing. A theme of speculative mania runs through his next two books: *Roughing It* (1872), which recalled his days in Nevada, and *The Gilded Age* (1873), which coined a name for the entrepreneurial days of post–Civil War America. The latter book was cowritten by Charles Dudley Warner, a fellow resident at Nook Farm.

In 1876, Twain published *The Adventures of Tom Sawyer*. Although not autobiographical in nature, the doings of Tom and Becky and the gang are indebted to Twain's own adolescence on the banks of the Mississippi.

Lecturing brought Twain to England next and two books were the result. The *Prince and the Pauper* (1882) and *A Connecticut Yankee in King Arthur's Court* (published several years later, in 1889). Both books portrayed a quintessentially American youth with a quintessential American sensibility stranded abroad. Twain would revisit the Mississippi again in 1883, but not his youth; he recalled his adult years as a riverboat pilot in the short story, "Life on the Mississippi."

Identity—whether transposed, in flux, or simply make-believe—and Americanness are threads running through Twain's mature work. In his intended sequel to *Tom Sawyer*, Twain seized onto this search for identity as a struggle for freedom, and mapped it squarely onto the geography of the Mississippi. He let his impersonal narrator go and gave the job instead to the American youth whose story it was to tell—Huck Finn, the uneducated son of the town drunk. In the story of Huck and his friend Jim, a runaway slave, Twain created a seminal work of fiction in a native American, distinctively Southern dialect. Ernest Hemingway stated what generations of readers were convinced of, that "All modern American literature comes from one book by Mark Twain called *Huckleberry Finn*. American writing comes from that. There is nothing before. There has been nothing as good since."

The *Adventures of Huckleberry Finn* (1884) was a pinnacle in Twain's career—not only as author, but as critic. In that book, Twain had attacked racism with irony. In the following years, he spoke out on themes of morality, religion, and politics while still, somehow, eliciting laughter.

After the Spanish-American War (1898), Twain became an ardent antiimperialist; he was especially critical of Belgium's role in the Congo and the policy of the United States in the Philippines. Twain was not always funny, and not always well received, but, he was always repeated. By the close of his career, the *New York Times* estimated that Twain was quoted in common conversation more often than any other American, including Ben Franklin and Abe Lincoln.

During the last fourteen years of his life, Twain suffered personally. He invested poorly in a new printing machine and, by 1894, he had lost most of his fortune. A world lecture tour helped him to restore a large portion of his earnings, but not his composure. As the years passed, Twain witnessed the premature deaths of his two daughters and, in 1904, the death of his wife, Livy. His writings took on an increasingly somber tone. Rather than poking fun at our foibles, he took brutal stabs at the human character. In *What Is Man?* (1906), Twain penned an exchange between the embittered man and young idealist that were, in truth, two incongruous parts of himself.

While many have taken Twain's darker fiction very seriously, in his autobiographical writings he makes himself the butt of his own joke. His autobiography is not a chronological account, but the ramblings of a man recollecting and commenting upon the story of his life as once told by his daughter, Suzy. The format is designed to offer up his own blameless, boyish nature for our amusement and edification. What becomes evident in these last writings is that he never lost his sagely ironic awareness, nor his capacity for rebound and affirmation.

Mark Twain died on 21 April 1910 just as he wanted—one day after the passing of Halley's Comet.